# THE SACRED indian TAROT

# THE SACRED indian TAROT

## SYMBOLS, IMAGES AND ICONS FROM INDIAN PHILOSOPHY

Kiren Rai

Om Books International

The Tree of Life

**The Tree of Life is perhaps the most widely recognised symbol or metaphor of the Tarot.**

*The Tree of Life provides a model for almost all systems of Western esoteric knowledge. In the Kabalah, the Tree of Life is visually a diagram of ten interconnected sephiroth or spheres. Twenty-two lines connect these spheres. Metaphorically, the spheres are divine emanations, which represent phases of human evolution. They radiate every force and factor of manifestation for the universe and human potential.*

*The Tree of Life has great mystical significance in Indian mythology. The Buddha received his illumination while under the Bodhi tree in India, and several of the Eastern gods are pictured sitting in meditation under a Bodhi tree. The Bodhi tree under which the Buddha achieved Enlightenment is a Peepal tree. The tree assumes special importance in the Indian tradition owing mainly to its 'two-way growth' ('roots' growing downwards for additional support). Traditional Buddhist records indicate that a branch of this tree was planted in Sri Lanka in the year 288 BC, and the tree is still alive today! There was a time in India when a Peepal tree was planted in the premises of every temple, and was regarded as sacred. Even today, the tree is held sacred by many and revered as an object of worship.*

*The symbolism of the tree is also mentioned in the 135th hymn of the tenth book of the* Rig Veda, *and in the fifteenth chapter of the* Bhagavad Gita. *Two varieties of the Fig (called* ashvatta *in Sanskrit), the Banyan tree and the Peepal tree are the most revered in the Indian tradition, and both are considered as highly auspicious. The Banyan symbolises fertility according to the* Agni Purana *and is worshipped by those wanting children. It is also referred to as the Tree of Immortality in many Hindu scriptures. The Banyan is believed to have nourished mankind with its 'milk' before the advent of grain and other food. The Fig tree is either a player or an observer in most Hindu ceremonies. Sages and seers sit under the shade of the Fig tree to seek enlightenment, hold discourses, and conduct Vedic rituals and the tree is mentioned in several scriptural references.*

## Acknowledgements

A special thanks to my team of artists and to Zoe Collington for so beautifully translating my thoughts into form.

Reprinted in 2024

**Om Books International**

Corporate & Editorial Office
A-12, Sector 64, Noida 201 301
Uttar Pradesh, India
Phone: +91 120 477 4100

Sales Office
4379/4B, Prakash House, Ansari Road
Darya Ganj, New Delhi 110 002, India
Phone: +91 11 2326 3363, 2326 5303
Fax: +91 11 2327 8091
Email: sales@ombooks.com
Website: www.ombooks.com



ISBN: 978-93-80070-12-4

10 9 8 7 6 5 4

Printed in India

# Table of Contents

CHAPTER 1

# Introduction to The Sacred Indian Tarot

*The Sacred Indian Tarot* is the first ever Indian book of tarot to combine the symbolism of the classic tarot with the aesthetic mastery of Indian culture and mythology. As an avid collector of tarot decks, I have an interesting collection put together over the years, from all over the world. I have around fifty tarot decks; my most treasured ones being a Chinese tarot deck with amazing artwork, an Egyptian book of tarots, the rare *Garuda* cards from Indonesia, and other such quaint decks.

On looking for an Indian deck of tarot cards, I could only find available the *Kama Sutra* cards and the Osho cards which are undoubtedly beautiful, but limited in their range. Considering that India has such a rich tradition of divination, I decided to put together an Indian book of tarot cards, using Indian images to represent the classic tarot prototypes. There is a strong similarity between the early tenets of tarot and the Hindu belief in *karma* as a regenerative process of consciousness. It is this metaphoric evolution of the human soul that makes the tarot such a popular oracle worldwide and which translates to form an integral part of *The Sacred Indian Tarot.*

*The Sacred Indian Tarot* is the first comprehensive Indian book of tarot cards based on Indian epics and mythology. The deck of cards contains 22 unique hand-painted cards with archetypes based on a rich tapestry of Indian images, stories, and symbols taken from the Mahabharata, Ramayana, *Bhagavad Gita*, and Upanishads. The structure and nomenclature of the Major Arcana remain the same; however the figures used to represent them are taken from Indian icons, symbols, and Indian epics, giving the subject an entirely Indian understanding.

So for instance, the High Priestess (II), second trump or Major Arcana card in most traditional tarot decks, is such a remarkable card symbolically that it is impossible to exhaust its symbolism. Perceived as a powerful intuitive feminine force, the High Priestess is the giver of life. In the Indian deck of cards, she has been represented by an Indian prototype, Shakti.

The Sanskrit word '*shakti*' can be translated as 'power' or 'energy'. It is derived from the verb root '*shak*,' which means 'to be able,' or 'to do,' or 'to act.' This power is witnessed in all the various phenomena of life. Shakti is the active, dynamic, feminine power, synonymous with the 'High Priestess' who manifests, sustains, and transforms the universe. In human beings, she is seen as the power of intelligence *(buddhi)*, compassion *(daya)*, and divine love *(bhakti)*, among her many other functions.

The Empress (III) represents the Mother in the Major Arcana. This woman is fertile with creative potential as she carries the future of humanity in her ripening womb. Shasthi, the Goddess of Fertility, fits primarily into this description. She is the great Mother Goddess of the world. She represents 'the eternal feminine'.

Likewise, Yama (XIII) represents the 'Death' card. Yama, like the Death card, personifies the consequences of mistaking our temporary delusions for our true selves. Yama was given the duties of custodian or protector of *dharma*. He is to uphold justice and is an adjudicator after death. *Dharma* is the law or way of the universe or cosmos.

The Fool (0) finds its prototype in the *Vidhushak*, the jestor, The Emperor (IV) in *Purusha*, the cosmic man, with a thousand heads, a thousand eyes, a thousand feet, and encompassing the earth, spreading in all directions into animate and inanimate things. Similarly the Sun (XIX) finds its correspondence in the all-powerful *Surya* and the illusionary Moon (XVIII) in *Chandrama* and various other such characterisations.

The major cards of the tarot consist of potent archetypes. An archetype is a model or pattern that is universal to the human experience. It also conveys significant energetic influences to and from the unconscious mind. Archetypes are part of the universal or collective unconscious. They affect us in many ways on many levels of our being, whether we are conscious of them or not. They appear in our thoughts, dreams, fantasies, and stories. They manifest themselves in our behaviour and in the people and situations around us.

Archetypes are represented by symbols. Some archetypes are characterised by human forms, such as the Great Mother, the Fool, and the Warrior. Archetypal symbols also take the form of objects such as the Wheel, the Cross, and the Tree. We can see these figures appearing over and over again in nature's creations as well as in our human creations.

It is helpful for us to be aware of how the archetypes work through us, so that we can understand these forces without allowing ourselves to be overcome by them. When we identify too strongly with an archetype, it overtakes us in thought and behaviour.

*The Sacred Indian Tarot* comes with a deck of 22 cards, an illustrated book with detailed interpretations of the Indian cards, along with a handout for doing the Indian *Karma* and *Chakra* tarot spreads. The book explains the significance of each archetype and its importance in the construction of the Indian deck of cards. The cards have been created by a group of upcoming Indian artists and the art form used is essentially the Bengal style of painting to depict images and icons from Indian mythology.

For the beginner, the book provides an exhaustive guide on how to use the tarot, complete with a basic guide to the meaning of each card.

CHAPTER 2

# UNIVERSALITY OF THE TAROT

## Indian Parallelism to The Tarot

Tarot *(Tar-oh)* is a system of symbolism and philosophy consisting of a set of 78 images. The origins of the tarot cards remain obscure. Although, the tarot first appeared historically in Europe during the Middle Ages, similar methods of divination existed in India and China.

The imagery of the tarot is replete with symbols that consist of potent archetypes universal to all religions. These archetypes are a part of every individual human mind and of the collective human consciousness. As we travel through the journey called life, we encounter events that fit into the symbolic archetypes relevant to all humans worldwide. So whether we speak of the Magician, the Lovers, the Wheel of Fortune, the Devil, the Sun, or the Star, the symbolism has many forms and many meanings for each student of divination. The tarot speaks many languages and its emblems and symbols are relevant to all cultures and religions. The cards are considered by some as parables of a Sufi master, Grail-related representations, Indian holy texts, Hebrew lore, Greek philosophy and of Kabalistic origin.

The history and origin of the cards are debatable and the doctrine behind these symbols has many overlaps and parallelisms between the East and the West. It is difficult to trace the origin of the tarot to any one country, region, or religion. Tarot is an anagram of *'Rota', Latin for *'the revolving wheel'*, its symbols consisting of potent archetypes that reflect the journey of life – the underlying pattern of the tarot is the journey of life from ignorance to a state of happiness.

---

*1856. Alphonse L. Constant, *Dogme et rituel de la haute magie*, vol. II, pp. 340–341. Constant suggests that the word 'Tarot' is an anagram of 'Rota', Latin for 'the revolving wheel', and found in a diagram accompanying Guillaume Postel's *Clavis Absconditorum* from 1582.

## Eastern Mysticism – A Bridge to The Tarot Cards

The mysteries of the tarot bear a relation to the spiritual principles of ancient India including the Vedas that contain esoteric concepts and have influenced religious traditions, art, beliefs, and knowledge throughout the ages, across the world. The images, symbols, structure, and concept of the tarot have a strong association with the Indian system of divination. The images and archetypes used in the deck of cards are similar to certain Indian astrological patterns and are strong enough to be seen even by a beginner.

## Tarot Cards are an Adaptation of Playing Cards

Let us begin with the structure of the tarot cards; the typical 78-card tarot deck is structured into two distinct parts. The first section consists of 22 cards and is known as the Trump cards or the Major Arcana.

The second section consists of 56 cards, divided into four suits and is known as the Minor Arcana. (Arcana is the plural form of the Latin word *'arcanum'*, meaning closed or secret.) The traditional tarot suits are Swords, Batons, Coins, and Cups. In modern tarot decks, the Batons suit is commonly called Wands, Rods, or Staves, while the Coins suit is often called Pentacles or Disks. The 14 cards in each suit consist of an ace, nine cards numbered 2 through 10, and four Court cards.

## Ganjifa and Playing Cards

Indian cards may have influenced the standard four suits prevalent in all tarot decks and also in a standard deck of cards. It is usually thought that tarot cards are different from normal ordinary playing cards. On the contrary, regular playing cards were indeed the predecessor to the tarot deck of cards.

Playing cards came to Europe from Islam, probably via Muslim Spain, much before the appearance of the tarots. They appeared quite suddenly in many different European cities between 1375 and 1378. European playing cards were an adaptation of the Islamic Mamluk cards in the late 1300s, by which time they had already assumed a form bearing close resemblance to those in use today.

Another important group of early Asian playing cards are the Ganjifa decks ('ganjifa' is of Persian origin) originally brought to India many centuries ago. It is not known whether these cards influenced the design of the Indian Ganjifa cards or vice versa. Round in shape, the early ones came in many sizes, styles and compositions, and were inspired by different themes, such as Lord Vishnu and the symbols of Vishnu's reincarnations, the planets, scenes from the Ramayana, etc.

One theory suggests that these Indian Ganjifa cards may have influenced the structure of a standard deck of card with its four suits. The four suits are also found in the 56 cards of the Minor Arcana, represented by the Wands, Cups, Swords, and Pentacles. This structure was then adapted by the tarot deck of cards and used for the purpose of divination.

GANJIFA CARDS

## THE MINOR TRUMPS AND THE CONCEPT OF THE FOUR HINDU ELEMENTS

To further highlight this association, the structure of the tarots – the Major Arcana, the Minor Arcana, and the Court cards can be traced to the four Vedas. The Vedas are the most comprehensive and universal of all ancient Indian scriptures. They have guided our religious lives for centuries and will continue to do so.

It has been suggested that the Minor Arcana is similar to the four Vedas, representing the more day-to-day, ritualistic aspects of Hindu life. The cards of the Minor Arcana are made up of four suits. These cards tell of the lesser events in our everyday lives and represent the different areas of life as depicted by the meaning of the Wands, Pentacles, Cups, and Swords.

The Major Arcana is more akin to the teachings of the Upanishads, which stand for the more powerful and spiritual principles of life. The Upanishads, like the Trumps, indicate self realisation and inspire people, engaged in the rituals of the Vedas, to go beyond their short-term goals and explore the greater meaning of life. The tarot Court cards, which give fresh meaning to the 16 'face' cards of the tarot, represent the King, Queen, Knight, and Page series. The courts cards of the Minor Arcana are actually elements within elements. They have a strong personal touch and reflect personal human attributes within the Minor Arcana based on the elements they represent.

The concept of elements is generally attributed to Indian origin. Accordingly, the human constitution is composed of four principles: spirit, soul, astral body, and the physical body. The spirit combines *atma* and *buddhi;* the soul includes *manas* and *kama;* the astral body is made up of both *prana* and *linga;* and the physical body is made up of *rupa.*

Each element has its prototype in the Court cards of the Minor Arcana. The Queen represents the soul; the Kings are emblems of the spirit; the Knights typify the astral body; and the Pages denote the physical body.

Looking at the Court cards with this perspective will help the tarot reader gain a better understanding of one of the more difficult aspects of the deck to reveal individuals in our lives and the roles they play in the form of the Court cards.

## GYPSIES POPULARISED THE TAROT IN EUROPE

The association of the tarot with India is further brought out with the connection of the cards with the gypsies. The gypsies whose actual homeland can be traced to India, left their native land and roamed across Europe and Asia. The gypsy religion tracks its beginnings to the Hindu religion, especially the worship of Kali, a female goddess of creation and destruction, one of the many manifestations of the World Mother or the Sacred Feminine. Though this theory is widely contended, the gypsies, however, may have been influential in promoting the divinatory use of the tarot in later centuries. Many theories and doctrines later, the tarot still remains a mysterious oracle; its emblems are full of meaning to every student of the ancient mysteries, no matter by what path he or she may have approached the truth. At the heart of them, the cards are an insight into the human mind.

## TAROT AND INDIAN SYMBOLISM

The language of the tarot is the symbols in the Arcana and these symbols are popular and prevalent in all religions. The journey of life, beginning from the Fool's journey to its completion in the World card, is common to the tenets of *karma* in Hindu mysticism. The tarot has a universal meaning; the underlying pattern of the tarot is the great journey of life from ignorance to the state of happiness.

As we go through the journey called life, we encounter various aspects and events that fit into these symbolic archetypes of the tarot. These archetypes are universal and common to humanity. Some of these symbols are specifically relevant to India, its traditions, its culture, and its religious imagery.

## Some Common Symbols

STAR OF DAVID

One of the most common symbols in the tarot imagery is the Star of David. As an archetypal symbol for the sacred union of the opposite energies, it can be considered the 'Yin-Yang' of Western civilisation.

SHATKONA

In India, the male-female union in the form of 'phallus' or '*shiva-linga*' or '*yoni-linga*' may be visualised as a parallel to this concept of polarity. The hexagon represents the *shatkona,* a combination of the *shivakona* (*trikona,* triangle), the symbol of Lord Shiva, representing the element of fire, and the *shaktikona,* representing the element of water. Together, they represent the union of male and female, and the perfect correspondence existing between the human being (seen as a true microcosm) and the creation as a whole (macrocosm).

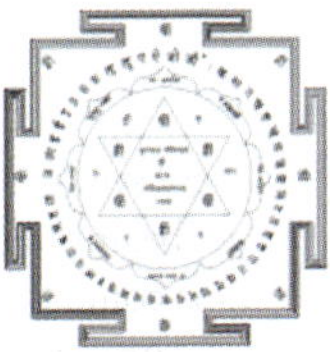

YANTRA

Another simple geometrical shape often used in the tarot is the circle, a universal symbol of unity, wholeness, and infinity. Further, in the complex symbolic system of Hinduism and

Buddhism, the *bindu* (dot) represents the male force. Together, the circle and the *bindu* symbolise the merging of male and female forces.

In the series of the five fundamental elements, the triangle (*Yantra*—geometric design used as a focus for meditation or devotional practice) represents forces that are even more intense than those generated by the simple forms. Buddhists utilise this geometric pattern in the *Sri Yantra mandala* as a tool to invoke the energy of love. Additionally, *Yantra* and *Mantra* are complementary aspects of Shiva and their use together is much more efficient than the use of one alone.

## * FEMININE ARCHETYPES ARE QUITE POWERFUL IN THE TAROT

THE CIRCLE AS WOMB

The World card, a card of completion can be understood as the 'cosmic dance' of Shiva and Shakti, a regular hexagram representing a man and a woman in intimate embrace. Aleister Crowley also points out to the Emperor as the male fiery energy of the universe and to the Kshatriya, *Rajas* of Hindu philosophy. The Emperor represents the swift creative energy, the initiative of all energy.

Similarly, the Empress represents the Mother. This woman is fertile with creative potential as she carries the future of humanity in her ripening womb. The Mother is indicating to us that we have already been fertilised

*The feminine archetypes are quite powerful in the tarot. I would like to refer to the way Aleister Crowley talked about Temperance, as an alchemical mixing of male and feminine. It is relative to the Hindu conceptions of Shiva and his partner Shakti (also called Kali or Durga), who combine to form the deity known as *Ardhnarishvara*, a being that is both feminine and masculine, a fusion of the two elements.

and are now gestating a new child, a new world, in our wombs. Shasthi, the Goddess of Fertility, fits primarily into this description. She is the Great Mother Goddess of the world. She represents 'the eternal feminine'.

In *The Sacred Indian Tarot,* Shakti is shown in her most terrifying manifestation – that of the vengeful goddess carrying the head of her enemy. However, Shakti has another persona – that of the gentle mother. One of the most recognised deities in the Hindu pantheon, Shakti is seen as both terrifying and beautiful by those who worship her. Also known as Durga, she is known to be a great celestial healer and has a softer side to her other terrifying self. So, too, does the typical High Priestess. She has (at least) two sides to her personality.

WHEEL OF FORTUNE

## WHEEL OF FORTUNE

The Wheel of Fortune relates to the *Bhavachakra,* the great Eastern symbol of the Solar Wheel and the *Ashok Chakra,* sometimes known as the sphere of birth and death, light and dark, and all the various pairs of opposites. Here, good and evil and pleasure and pain are inseparable.

TREE OF LIFE

## TREE OF LIFE

Similarly, the Tree of Life has great significance in Hindu mythology. The Buddha received his enlightenment under the Bodhi tree in India, and several of the Eastern gods are depicted sitting in meditation under a Bodhi Tree. The rose and the lotus represent spiritual enlightenment and attainment. Hence, the Eastern deities are often shown seated on open petals of the lotus.

An incredible number of other mystical systems can also accurately correspond to the tarot such as Astrology, Kabalah, Runes, and I Ching. While this may indicate a common history with some of these systems, I believe it points to the universality and truths inherent in them all.

CHAPTER 3

# THE MAJOR ARCANA

*The Sacred Indian Tarot* is a set of cards, comprising the first 22 archetypal cards (0-21), the High Arcana, based on the cosmic laws of *karma* that deal with the principal questions of the self and its relation to the Absolute. The High Arcana is the 'fate cards' that form the mainstay of Indian philosophy.

The images on the Major Arcana are often very heavy with symbolism, with far more to the illustration than a mere depiction of the card title. The Major Arcana is usually regarded as relating to matters of higher purpose or deep significance, as opposed to the Minor Arcana which relate to the everyday world and matters of immediate significance. Major Arcana cards give insights about behaviour or events through their powerful symbolism. They represent the state of being in terms of mental, emotional, or spiritual condition at the time of the reading.

These Arcana cards are numbered from 1 to 21. The only unnumbered one is the Fool. An interesting card, it is a key of 0 and yet a key of 22 as well. There are 22 cards to the Major Arcana, starting with number 1-21. The number 22 would seem to be missing if we just called it 0. The 0 key represents the God force, the force before entering into manifestation, but in the same right, this card completes the cycle as number 22. Life continues on and on in a cycle and the number 22 is an ancient symbol for a circle representing God and infinity, because a circle has no starting point or end.

The cards of the Major Arcana consisting of archetypes refer to spiritual matters and important trends in the querent's life.

An archetype has both a positive and a negative side. For example, the Devil card in the tarot is often viewed as a negative influence in a reading. However, it does have its positive side, because it shows us aspects of ourselves and our lives that we need to be aware of and either change or integrate. At the same time, a card such as the Star traditionally has a positive connotation. Yet, it too has its negative side, in that, it may convey to the querent that he is setting his sights too high, or that he is dreaming of a goal that he is not following through. It is enlightening to discover the tarot and to use the cards for self-awareness and decision making.

— 0 —

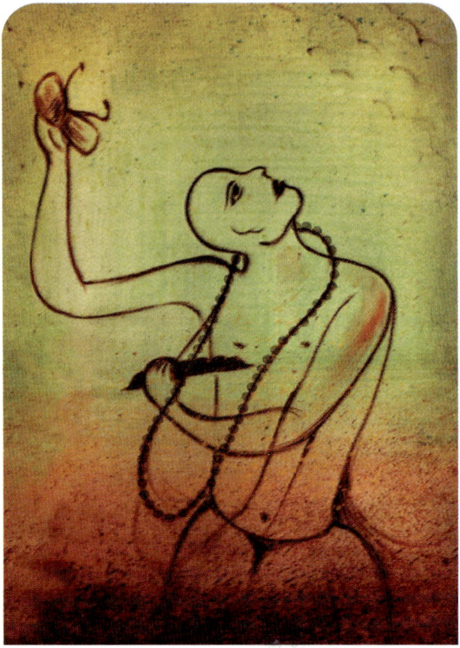

THE FOOL • vidhushak

*This handmade sketch of the* vidhushak *has been inspired by the character of a* natgiri, *a wandering minstrel, in Indian folk stories. The* vidhushak *is an expression of cheerful exuberance and his short life (in cosmic time) is a celebration of the now. However, on a more serious note, the* vidhushak *also embodies the voice of question and his theatrical performances are an attempt to bring out the burning social issues one is confronted with every day.*

# THE FOOL • vidhushak (0)

## THE CARD – THE INTERPRETATION

*Vidhushak* / the Fool is an interesting archetype that marks the beginning of the life journey culminating in the World card. The Fool is a spirit in search of an experience. Its journey stands for new beginnings, spontaneity, optimism, purity of purpose, and an unconventional thought process. The Fool symbolises a journey into the self, represented by the 21 additional cards of the Major Arcana, the so-called 'triumphs' *(i.e., 'Trumps')* of the journey.

## REVERSED

This card indicates problems that may arise from extreme restlessness, ill-considered decisions, confusion, and poor application of life energies. Lack of focus, apathy, and single-mindedness can lead to trouble. Symbolically, the fool can be understood as one who is naïve and lacking in forethought. Discipline and grounding are needed to achieve your life purpose ...

## VIDHUSHAK – THE SAGA

The *Vidhushak* is a blend of 'the clown of Sanskrit plays and a folk performer in Indian mythology'. The *Vidhushak* is a *natgiri*, a vagabond, yet a wise character who delivers a constructive message to society in a light and spiritual vein. *Vidhushak* / the Fool is the first card of the Major Arcana and at a symbolic level, this archetype represents a spiritual life journey beginning at the base level of physical survival to lessons in self-empowerment, self-discovery, generosity, compassion, and self-esteem. The journey is one's path, one's destiny, and one's life.

*An interesting deviation in this deck is that the Magician has been represented by a female figure, in the form of* Usha, *the Goddess of Dawn.* Usha *represents the strong feminine symbolism that is an integral part of Indian tradition. The goddess understands that rebirth occurs in each moment and her halo in the painting is a symbol of infinity that shows the cosmic connection to all things in the universe.*

# The Magician ▪ उषा (I)

## The Card – The Interpretation

*Usha* / the Magician (I) is the first trump card of the Major Arcana. The Magician is the master of its own destiny. It wears a halo, a symbol of infinity, which shows the cosmic connection to all things, above and below. The card indicates that if you want to achieve your highest possible destiny, become a conjurer of sorts to yourself. You have the intelligence, knowledge, strength, resources, and organisational skills to make your dreams come true. By setting specific and attainable goals, the Magician utilises its great knowledge and wisdom to succeed where others have failed.

## Reversed

This card indicates an inability to deal with changes that could lead to new and better things. There is a desire and hope of greater happiness; however you need to challenge the inertia within yourself and tap into your potential to fulfil your destiny. Guidance can arrive through one's own intuition or in the form of someone who brings about change or transformation.

## Usha – The Saga

*Usha,* the Goddess of Dawn, is the daughter of Heaven, and heralds the arrival of the Sun in her golden chariot yoked by seven ruddy horses. She is the life and health of all things, being born every day and yet she is an immortal being. *Usha* is considered a medium of awakening. Dawn is said to be the archetype that symbolises truth and clarity. She signifies supreme illumination as she rises with the radiance of her truth.

— II —

THE HIGH PRIESTESS ▪ Shakti

*This handmade painting depicts the fight between Durga and Mahishasura. Durga is the warrior aspect of the divine Mother (Shakti), an embodiment of creative feminine force. According to a legend, the gods could not defeat the buffalo demon Mahishasura, who was threatening the existence of the universe. They begged Shiva for his assistance, and Shiva advised all the gods to release their* shaktis. *The* shaktis *of the gods emerged in female form. Thus armed, Durga rode, defeated Mahishasura and his army of demons, and thus saved the universe from this demon's menace.*

# THE HIGH PRIESTESS ▪ शक्ति (II)

## THE CARD – THE INTERPRETATION

*Shakti* / the High Priestess (II) is the second trump or Major Arcana card in most traditional tarot decks and rules the intuitive human faculties. The card helps us to relate to our sixth sense, gaining insights and answers in an intuitive and subtle way. When she appears in a spread, she counsels you to seek new and hidden paths to wisdom.

## REVERSED

You are on a path of exploration; do not become distracted. The card can also be a warning to interrogate the lessons of the unconscious and differentiate between fantasy and reality.

## SHAKTI – THE SAGA

*Shakti* is synonymous with the Devi, or divine power that manifests, sustains, and transforms the universe. *Shakti* represents the active, dynamic principles of feminine power. She is the sacred force, power, or energy in the Hindu concept or personification of the divine feminine aspect, sometimes referred to as 'the Divine Mother'. The grace of *Shakti* showers boons of strength, peace, wisdom, and prosperity whereas its absence leads to destitution, hopelessness, pain, and misery.

— III —

THE EMPRESS ▪ shasthi

*Shasthi is a Hindu Goddess of Fertility and Childbirth, worshipped all over India and in other parts of the world. In this painting, she has been shown with a child in her womb, seated on a bed of lotus flowers with a halo around her head that radiates energy, abundance, fertility, and creativity.*

# THE EMPRESS ▪ षष्ठी (III)

## THE CARD – THE INTERPRETATION

*Shasthi* / the Empress represents a female form associated with fertility, growth, abundance, knowledge, wealth, domestic stability, and happiness. The Empress is the embodiment of womanhood and symbolises one-half of a perfect polarity – the Emperor being the other side of the balance. At her highest level, the Empress also represents the Great Mother in her aspect of protector, nurturer, teacher, lover, and friend. The card is a card of promise and opportunity. The Empress brings a flood of hope and is the epitome of abundance.

## REVERSED

This card indicates a need to reconsider the ways in which we express love and receive love in our lives. Introspect and be aware of the human capacity to love and create, as well as to hate and destroy.

## SHASTHI – THE SAGA

*Shasthi* is the goddess for gifting children. She is the protectress of children and her mount is a cat. She is gold skinned with a child in her arms and in vermilion hue. Since she also represents the Great Mother, all the elements of compassion, unconditional love, and acceptance come to the forefront, fulfilling her part in the eternal cycle of creation.

— IV —

THE EMPEROR ▪ purusha

*The card represents a crowned male figure, an embodiment of virtue, strength, and love, sitting on the imperial throne attired in imperial vestments and regalia. The Emperor is one of the more important alchemical cards and with Atu II (The High Priestess) and III (The Empress), he makes up the triad: Sulphur, Mercury, and Salt. Sulphur is the male fiery energy which in the Hindu system corresponds to the three Gunas–Sattva, Rajas, and Tamas. The Gunas are represented in European philosophy by the three qualities, Sulphur, Mercury, and Salt.*

# THE EMPEROR • purusha (IV)

## THE CARD – THE INTERPRETATION

*Purusha* / the Emperor card is of a person in natural possession of logic, power, and authority. The card indicates an inherent leadership quality that will help you to accomplish and fulfil all that you desire. A card of authority, you will overcome all obstacles to attract prosperity and balance. You are disciplined and better able to deal with change that will lead to new and better things.

## REVERSED

If reversed, the card indicates a strong streak of distrust, and lack of responsibility. Take a good look at the situation and rely only on yourself to see a way through the situation. Pay heed to your organisational skills. This will help you stay grounded and focussed.

## PURUSHA – THE SAGA

In Hindu mythology, *Purusha* is the cosmic man, with a thousand heads, a thousand eyes, a thousand feet encompassing the earth, spreading in all directions into animate and inanimate things. *Purusha* is described as a primeval giant, sacrificed by the gods and from whose body the world and the *varnas* (castes) are built. In Indian philosophy, the spark of life in each individual is called the *Purusha,* in whose presence, the matter constituting *prakriti* becomes vitalised.

NOTE: See *Purus* and *Prakriti* (the lovers) for a deeper understanding of *Purusha.*

— V —

THE HIEROPHANT ▪ atman

*This handmade painting represents a human being who through consistent yogic practice and meditation has aligned and balanced the energy vortices that are the seven chakras in our physical bodies. When the chakras come into alignment, the energy available to them increases and the individual can then experience a more meaningful and fulfilling life experience.*

# THE HIEROPHANT ▪ atman (V)

## THE CARD – THE INTERPRETATION

In the highest spiritual context, the Hierophant represents a human being who has united all aspects of duality, evolving to a point of high development and growth. The merging of earth-water-fire-air-ether leads to the pursuit of knowledge and truth. On a more day-to-day context, the card allows for free communication, artistic expression, good judgement, self-belief, wisdom, and knowledge in day–to-day activities.

## REVERSED

An imbalance in the energy flow can make one inflexible, dominating, and egotistical causing a self-righteous attitude. The card is a wake-up call to awaken the Hierophant, the spiritual teacher, or the divine light within. A Hierophant can be a teacher you seek or can be your own inner spiritual teacher.

## ATMAN – THE SAGA

The *atman* is a philosophical term used in Hinduism to identify the soul. Atman is the individual soul in essence, but also a microscopic form of the absolute universality – that which is *Brahman.* The *atman* can ascend beyond the current realms when freed from all restraints of the mind and body. Vedic literature suggests that there is a single essence *(Brahman)* that underlies all existence and animates all living beings. A person's realisation of the identity and unity of *atman* and *Brahman* is believed to bring about liberation.

— VI —

THE LOVERS ▪ purus and prakriti

*In Hindu mythology, the eternal love of Radha and Krishna remains the greatest love story ever. Krishna is depicted alongside Radha, his gopi consort, frolicking in the village of Vrindavan during his childhood. Radha-Krishna also symbolises the union of* purus *and* prakriti*, the eternal love relation between the individual and the divine.*

# THE LOVERS • purus and prakriti (VI)

## THE CARD – THE INTERPRETATION

The Lovers indicate harmonisation of opposites at all levels of being. Symbolically, the card indicates a union of the male and female. Where you do not have a partner or a relationship with others, the card helps you to resolve your own inner struggles to realise and fulfil your needs. On a more day-to-day basis, a partnership is in the offing; perhaps a choice needs to be made, a reminder that balance is essential in all relationships.

## REVERSED

If reversed, the card indicates a negative relationship, contradictions in partnerships, and a destructive state. This card focuses on your relationships, a moral and emotional dilemma, and the need to exercise a correct choice.

## PURUS AND PRAKRITI – THE SAGA

Radha and Krishna are the eternal lovers that symbolise the union of *purus* and *prakriti*. The man *(purush)* is symbolic of the conscious mind and the woman *(prakriti)* of the unconscious connected to the divine source. '*Purus*' is a term in Indian philosophy denoting the individual conscious principle. *Prakriti* is primordial in nature; the material substratum of creation, consisting of *Sattva*, *Rajas*, and the *Tamas gunas*. It is through the woman that a man achieves his connection to God, or the Higher Self. This is a union of reciprocation and harmonious love, a balance between the conscious and the unconscious.

— VII —

THE CHARIOT ▪ rath

*The Mahabharata is the longest epic ever composed and is a common subject for representation in Indian art and culture. The scene depicted here is of Krishna, the charioteer* (sarathi), *delivering a life lesson to Arjuna, as the two sides (Pandavas* and *Kauravas) are poised for battle on the battlefield of Kurukshetra. Krishna's address to Arjuna forms the heart of the spiritual teachings of the* Bhagavad Gita, *a Sanskrit text from the chapter* 'Bhishma Parva' *of the Mahabharata.*

# THE CHARIOT • रथ (VII)

## THE CARD – THE INTERPRETATION

*Rath* / the Chariot is a card which contains great dynamism, strength, and power. Often, when it comes in a reading, it indicates the struggles we have with ourselves and with life. The card is very motivating as it indicates that the querent has successfully integrated the life lessons of the first six cards and will move towards balance and harmony. It also indicates positive changes that will be beneficial and bring triumph and success with them.

## REVERSED

You are overwhelmed with the effort as you have struggled through a difficult and demanding time, battling against long odds to achieve the things that we need out of life. Allow yourself to look within and reclaim the balance, your own power and to move forward with self-confidence.

## RATH – THE SAGA

The sermon of the *Bhagavad Gita* was given over five thousand years ago on the battlefield of Kurukshetra by Lord Krishna to Arjuna. The world is a stage and the real Kurukshetra is within you. The battle of Mahabharata is still raging within you. Ignorance *(avidya)* is Dhritarashtra. The individual soul is Arjuna. The dweller who dwells in your heart is Lord Krishna, the charioteer. The body is your chariot. The senses (*Indriyas*) are the horses. The ultimate essence of the chariot is that the soul *(jiva)* should unwarrantedly conquer the mind, senses, *vasanas*, and egoism, if it is to successfully traverse the journey *(yatra)* of life, *samsara* to a God-realised state.

— VIII —

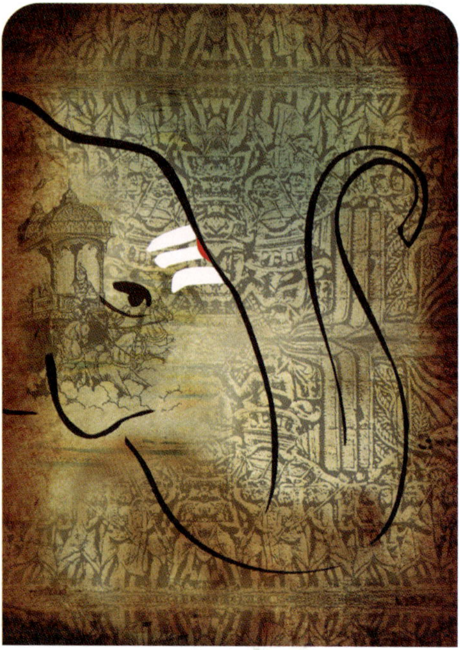

STRENGTH ▪ bhima

*This is a very famous scene from the epic, the Mahabharata. The name Bhima brings to mind images of a young, strong prince, equally well known for his physical strength, as he was for his strength of character. The eye of the elephant opens to the battlefields of Kurukshetra, where the Kauravas and the Pandavas fought the epic battle described in the Mahabharata.*

# STRENGTH • bhima (VIII)

## THE CARD – THE INTERPRETATION

*Bhima* / Strength denotes a strong personal character with high self-worth and confidence and is the very foundation of the physical body. The card indicates qualities of perseverance, courage, resolve, and inner strength that will see you through your hardest times. It also indicates an ability to relate to others in an open and friendly way and to deal with life to the best of your ability.

## REVERSED

It means being weak, full of fears, and being plagued by fantasies. If this card is reversed, it may lead to you feeling emotionally explosive and manipulated. The card is about exercising self-discipline, courage, and creativity to overcome any hardship that you may face.

## BHIMA – THE SAGA

In the epic battle described in the Mahabharata, *Bhima* is a legendary figure, a giant in physical strength, whose legendary prowess have been mentioned throughout the epic: 'of all the wielders of the mace, there is none equal to *Bhima*'. In fight, it is said: 'He yields not to even Arjuna; and as to might of arms, he is equal to ten thousand elephants.' *Bhima* was a pivotal figure in the great battle of Kurukshetra and his charioteer was Lord Krishna's son. *Bhima* was bestowed with a great mind and was supposed to be a strategist with superhuman strength. The Pandavas also represent the inherent goodness manifest in all human beings.

— IX —

THE HERMIT ▪ rishi

*In ancient India,* rishis *were enlightened beings who turned inwards for self-realisation and discovered the mysteries of life. In the Vedic age,* rishis *lived in forest or mountain retreats, either alone or with disciples.* Rishis *were great souls who were the preceptors of the sacred hymns of the Vedas. Seven particular* rishis *(the* saptarishis*) mentioned in the Rig Veda are said to be the original seers and who still guide mankind from the inner worlds.*

# THE HERMIT ▪ ṛiṣhi (IX)

## THE CARD – THE INTERPRETATION

*Rishi* / the Hermit is a spiritual and reassuring card, for he symbolises withdrawal into one's own centre point, where the directions of the still inner voice may be clearly heard. In a reading, the Hermit often suggests a need for time alone – a period of reflection when distractions are limited. The Hermit stands for the still centre that must be created for balance and harmony. In a reading, the Hermit can represent a quest for deeper understanding or the truth of a situation.

## REVERSED

When you get this card in a reading, it can indicate a need to withdraw, to take stock, and review your life. It can also indicate a preoccupation with details, a need to finding a teacher, or guide, or being a guide for others.

## RISHI – THE SAGA

In Hinduism, a *rishi* is a sage and/or seer who 'heard' the hymns of the Vedas from the supreme being – *Brahman* – while he was in deep meditation. A *rishi* can be regarded as a combination of a patriarch, a priest, a preceptor, an author of Vedic hymns, a sage, a saint, and an ascetic. The *rishi* stands alone on the silent, white mountaintop and the divine light illuminates the path of ascent.

—X—

THE WHEEL OF FORTUNE ▪ dharma

*The Wheel of Dharma is a common symbol of Buddhist teachings represented in the form of a wheel usually with eight spokes which represent the eight-fold path. The teachings, like a wheel, are thought to be eternal in having neither a beginning nor an end. The shape of the wheel conveys the completeness and faultlessness of the* dharma *teaching.*

# THE WHEEL OF FORTUNE ▪ dharma (X)

## THE CARD – THE INTERPRETATION

When *Dharma* / the Wheel of Fortune appears in a spread, it indicates the beginning of a new cycle, a new beginning of events, a time for positivity, and karmic change. There is also a sense of understanding, completeness, and a feeling of being at complete peace with oneself. A change for the better, the unfolding future holds much promise.

## REVERSED

You are on the path of awareness. A setback or streak of bad luck is indicated. Patience and timing will resolve most of these issues. Avoid taking foolish chances and learn from your mistakes.

## DHARMA CHAKRAS – THE SAGA

The Wheel of Fortune also symbolises the concept of *karma*; the *Dharma Chakra* (wheel) is also sometimes translated as Wheel of Doctrine or the Wheel of Law. The *Dharma Chakra* from the Lion Capital of Asoka, at Sarnath, is the national emblem of India and is also shown on the flag of India. It represents the *dharma*, *i.e.*, natural conduct of a nation. The Wheel's motion is a metaphor for the endless cycle of *samsara*, or rebirth, which can only be escaped by means of the Buddha's teachings – the eight-fold path leading to enlightenment. It is drawn from an Indian symbol, but instead of representing *samsara*, or endless rebirth, it symbolises overcoming obstacles.

— XI —

JUSTICE ▪ nyaya

*Namaskaram is a common spoken greeting or salutation in the Indian subcontinent. It is derived from Hinduism and Buddhism, and is a gesture of folded hands commonly used in day-to-day life. Translated in simple usage, it means 'I bow to you in humble salutation.' In tarot formulation, it can be translated as respect for the divine for rendering ultimate justice in the universe.*

# JUSTICE ▪ nyaya (XI)

## THE CARD – THE INTERPRETATION

*Nyaya* / Justice is a card that calls for self-assessment, which will help you experience completeness within and with the universe. In a more mundane sense, this card may signal a court case, legal documents, and adjustments in a marriage or partnership. The outcome of all these may not be exactly what the querent wants, but it will be a scrupulously fair outcome.

## REVERSED

When we fail to consistently assess our position and attitudes in relation to life, in general and on a personal level, we too begin to stagnate. In practice, the Justice card symbolises *karmic* retribution and lessons that need to be learnt in a more difficult way. It, therefore, represents both the law of the universe and that of cause and effect. The card calls for using the intellect to resolve any imbalance within us.

## NYAYA – THE SAGA

*Nyaya* or Hindu logic was founded by Gautama Rishi, who is also known by the names Akshapada and Dirghatapas. *Nyaya* is an analytic type of philosophy. The word *'nyaya'* signifies going into a subject, *i.e.*, investigating it analytically. In this sense of analysis, the word *'nyaya'* is exactly opposed to *sankhya*, synthesis. *Nyaya* is sometimes called *Tarka-Vidya* or the Science of Debate, *Vada-Vidya* or the Science of Discussion. *Tarka* is the special feature of the *nyaya*.

*In India, to dream of a rope noose indicates an unfortunate personal entanglement that will entail some difficulty to loosen. To dream of a noose hanging from a tree denotes fear and anxiety. Metaphorically, the noose can be used for ensnaring or binding the individual ego so as to attain absolute detachment from all worldly ties.*

# THE HANGED MAN ▪ tyaga (XII)

## THE CARD – THE INTERPRETATION

*Tyaga* / The Hanged Man often indicates a period of apparent inertia as an opportunity for self-development, where new concepts are being absorbed. This card denotes a time when everything stands still, a time for reflection before moving on. Things will continue, but for now, they float, timeless. It is also a time of letting go, renouncing a claim, suspension, giving up control, and accepting God's will.

## REVERSED

The Hanged Man signals a need to retreat in order to achieve what you want. It can also signal a refusal to accept reality. This card can also show that it is time for you to look at the situation from another angle. Issues will become clear, solutions to problems found. Stop resisting or opposing and in doing so you will gain eventually.

## TYAGA – THE SAGA

*Tyaga* or renunciation in Hindu mythology denotes a gradual dissociation from worldly objects and from the seed of desire. This renunciation is not a renunciation of something material but something closer to the notion of ascetic renunciation. *Tyaga* also involves giving up on the fruit of action and performing *karma* without expecting any fruit for such action. Sri Krishna has explained that renunciation is greater than asceticism, to remember God and do ones appointed work without desire is far greater than the freedom to do as one likes. Renunciation means renunciation of desire and renunciation of selfishness.

— XIII —

DEATH ▪ yama

*The theme of this painting is the depiction of the Hindu God of Death, armed with a noose as well as a club, riding his black buffalo. In Hindu mythology,* Yama *judges and perpetuates souls.* Yama *is also the Lord of Justice and is sometimes referred to as* Dharma. *He drags the souls of the condemned out of the bodies to judge them.*

# DEATH • yama (XIII)

## THE CARD – THE INTERPRETATION

*Yama* / Death is the 13th Trump or Major Arcana card. The Death card does not mean physical death. Rather, the Death card portrays symbolic death, a change, or transformation. Often, it heralds the end of a familiar or more comfortable mode. It conveys a release, casting of the past, looking to the future, transformation, a turning point, change of personality, complete change in one's way of life and circumstances, or a new cycle of events.

## REVERSED

Ungrounded, the card signifies a difficult transition, a prolonged upheaval or an unpleasant change. Perhaps it even brings a whole new set of principles which will guide you spiritually, emotionally, psychologically, and help you to break new grounds.

## YAMA – THE SAGA

*Yama* is the God of Death and the embodiment of the rule of law, and imparts justice according to the deeds of each person. He is to uphold justice and is an adjudicator after death. With the duties of God of Death, he was also given the duties of custodian or protector of *Dharma. Dharma* is the law or way of the universe or cosmos. With this extra duty, he was given the title of *Dharma-Raja* or the Lord of *Dharma.*

— XIV —

TEMPERANCE ▪ ardhnarishvara

Ardhnarishvara *is one of the most prevalent forms of Indian art in the last several thousand years. The left part of the image is female and the right is male, depicting Shiva and his consort Shakti/Parvati. Like in the unity of* Ardhnarishvara, *all opposites are reconciled. This card can often be interpreted as a need for blending or synthesising the opposites.*

# TEMPERANCE ▪ ardhnarishvara (XIV)

## THE CARD – THE INTERPRETATION

*Ardhnarishvara* / Temperance is a card of harmony, and its appearance shows that your inner power is ready to heal and make you stronger. Taken literally, temperance means finding the middle ground, showing moderation, experiencing harmony, and balance. This is a strong card indicating that you are able to wield your own strength to attract prosperity and success.

## REVERSED

Before you can achieve harmony in your relationships with the people around you, you must make peace with yourself. In addition to its literal meaning of temperance or moderation, the Temperance card can often be interpreted as a need for blending the opposites within you.

## ARDHNARISHVARA – THE SAGA

In Sanskrit, *Ardhnarishvara* means 'half-female Lord.' Lord Shiva in an androgynous form is considered as male on the right side and female on the left. Shiva is genderless and inseparable from his female energy. It is conjectured that by wresting from her husband, one-half of his body as her own, and mingling in his physical frame, Parvati obtained an ideal, archetypal union with her husband. *Ardhnarishvara* is a perfect master of the two contrary elements in the manifest universe. In Shiva, the *ida* (feminine) and the *pingala* (masculine) *nadis* (psychic nerve currents) are balanced so that *sushumna* (flow of *kundalini*) is ever active. In the unity of *Ardhnarishvara*, all opposites are reconciled as any duality fades away into the one source.

— XV —

THE DEVIL ▪ asura

*Asuras are depicted as half-human, half-snake-like divine beings with exaggerated features in Indian mythology. Asuras as opposed to Devas were power-seeking deities often with a sinful or evil trait of character. In today's Hinduism, Asuras are demons, but this was not always the case. The idea of Asuras is very old. Asuras only became demons as time passed and they began to lose their divine goodness.*

# THE DEVIL • asura (XV)

## THE CARD – THE INTERPRETATION

Bound to a particular idea, material obsession and manipulation of power, *Asura* / the Devil card is a wake-up call and acts as a warning to you of the dangers of being wrapped up in anything that is unhealthy—relationships, habits, and situations.

## REVERSED

The Devil is a card of self-bondage to an idea, or belief, which prevents a person from growing or being healthy. The Devil more accurately represents our bondage to material things rather than to any evil persona. It also indicates an obsession or addiction to fulfilling our own earthly base desires. Should the Devil represent a person, it will most likely be the one who is persuasive, aggressive, and controlling.

## ASURA – THE SAGA

*Asura* in Indian mythology represents a 'power-seeking' and 'power-hungry' demon. The *Danavas*, *Asuras*, and *Daityas* are synonyms to this concept. Indian *Asuras* were part of the Vedic culture and descendents of kings and sages; they were not necessarily evil but had certain character flaws that lead to their downfall. Symbolically, *Asuras*' horns refer to being in the clutches of egotistical behaviour, the snake in the *Asura* represents Nahusha, who became drunk with power and was turned into a serpent – a creature of darkness unable to see the light. The *Asura*'s head is an exaggeration of sorts reminding us not to take ourselves too seriously.

— XVI —

THE TOWER ▪ kila

*The painting depicts a Kila, a medieval structure that provided a vantage point for the ruling class in ancient India. The minars and forts of India are famous for their rich history and architectural magnificence.*

# THE TOWER • किला (XVI)

## THE CARD – THE INTERPRETATION

*Kila* / the Tower may bring in unexpected change, a sudden shift in perceptions, a burst of insight, a seeing through illusions, or plans being disrupted. Disillusionment and confusion are natural reactions to the Tower card; however, the overthrow of an old way of life may lead to true enlightenment ahead.

## REVERSED

The Tower card immediately follows the Devil card, revealing after the self-bondage of the Devil, the Tower is a self-correcting card. The Tower shows us a basic fact of spiritual life change, brings growth, and the querent will be forced to take a new direction. A reassessment of current beliefs may actually help you reach a new level of understanding.

## KILA – THE SAGA

A *Kila* is a fortress in ancient literature of India. *Kila*s were normally situated on surmountable hilltops and stood like bastions against the enemy forces. A tower is often a phallic symbol of materialism, pride, imprisonment, patriarchy, false institutions, false power, false protection, and dominant supremacy.

XVII

THE STAR • tara

Tara *is shown here as the feminine counterpart of the* bodhisattva *('Buddha-to-be'), the great compassionate mother, the star of heaven.* Tara *is an archetype of our own inner wisdom. She is the goddess of transformation, of consciousness, a journey to freedom. Each person must discover within themselves the wisdom, compassion, and glory that is* Tara.

# THE STAR • tara (XVII)

## THE CARD – THE INTERPRETATION

*Tara* / the Star is the best card in the entire deck, in my opinion. It marks a point where fortune smiles upon us, lighting up our dreams, hopes and wishes with the promise of fulfilment and manifestation. There are few cards more positive than the Star, because when it appears in your life, it is nothing less than a beacon of hope and inspiration.

## REVERSED

In times of darkness, it shows that there is a way out, and tells you not to worry, for illumination and freedom are at hand. All you need is something in which to place your faith. So trust in yourself, and in whatever powers you believe control the universe, to help you through difficult times. Let the infinite energy of the Star warm you and rejuvenate your soul, to provide the strength and the clarity of purpose you need to continue on your journey.

## TARA – THE SAGA

*Tara* is a Sanskrit word, meaning 'star'. We hear echoes of her name in the Latin *'Terra'* (Mother Earth). The goddess of universal compassion, *Tara* represents virtuous and enlightened action. It is said that her compassion for living beings is stronger than a mother's love for her children. She also brings about longevity, protects earthly travel, and guards her followers on their spiritual journey to enlightenment.

— XVIII —

THE MOON ▪ chandra

*In India, a* Moti Chandrama *pendant is worn to provide powerful protection against a debilitated moon in your planetary chart. The pearl is worn to harmonise the moon which directly influences the seasonal, monthly, and daily cycles and rhythms of our physiology and emotions. Wearing a pearl pendant can bring stability to these influences and gather auspicious energies to appease the planet Moon.*

# THE MOON • chandra (XVIII)

## THE CARD – THE INTERPRETATION

You need to keep your eyes open with this card. *Chandra* / the Moon card indicates duality; it also shows illusion, deception, and uncertainty. The moon has a habit of casting things and experiences in a different light. Things are not quite how they seem, be wary of the illusion created by the Moon.

## REVERSED

This indicates indulgence in fantasies, losing direction and purpose, having unrealistic ideas, misapprehending the truth and letting your imagination rule your mind. Rather than escaping into delusion and losing control of reality, give form to this imagery by developing your creative and psychic powers.

## MOON – THE SAGA

*Soma* is the Moon God also known as *Chandra*. According to a legend, *Surya* nourishes the moon with water from the ocean when *Soma* is exhausted by the many beings that feed upon its substance. It is believed that during half the month, thirty-six thousand divinities feed on *Soma* and thus assure their immortality. This account neatly combines the two aspects of *Soma*, as the nectar from which the gods derive their strength and as the moon that waxes and wanes. The legend of the banishment of *Soma* by Brahma to the outer atmosphere can be interpreted as yet another myth explaining how intoxicants came to be banned.

— XIX —

THE SUN • Surya

*Hindus have revered the sun, which they call* Surya, *as both the physical and spiritual heart of the world and the creator of all life itself. The card* Surya *depicts a powerful means of honouring the sun through the dynamic yoga sequences –* suryanamaskaram, *better known as sun salutation.*

# THE SUN • surya (XIX)

## THE CARD – THE INTERPRETATION

When *Surya* / the Sun shines on you, it provides new ways of resolving problems, new perspectives, and fresh viewpoints. Glory, gains, riches, confidence, strength, and self-assurance abound within. You are in a state of equanimity and well-being for the sun brings in abundance, achievement, joy, and happiness.

## SURYA – THE SAGA

In Hindu mythology, *Surya* is the Lord of Excellence and Wisdom. Even today, people place the symbol of the sun over their shops because they think it will bring good fortune. The Sun God, who is also known as Narayana, or Vishnu, the soul of all the worlds, is situated in outer space between the upper and lower portions of the universe. The sun represents well-being itself. In India, all rituals are sun-centred. *Suryanamaskar* (an ancient Indian yoga) is the art of solar vitalisation. It is a complete meditative technique in itself as it includes *asanas*, *pranayama*, *mantras*, and *mudras*. It has got three aspects: form, vital energy, and rhythm.

— XX —

THE JUDGEMENT ▪ jyothi

*This image depicts the Buddha sitting in a meditative posture on a lotus blossom that symbolises self-realisation. The symbol of the Buddha holds many meanings. It conveys a calm positive mind that reflects mental discipline and positive thoughts. It is also a way to connect to the divinity in all living things.*

# THE JUDGEMENT• jyothi (XX)

## THE CARD – THE INTERPRETATION

*Jyothi* / The Judgement card comes up in a reading when we are at crossroads and it is a time to resurrect a new phase of life. It comes at a pivotal time when we must be honest with ourselves and rise up to the challenges of life. Judgement signifies the start of a new journey, guided by lessons learnt in the past. It represents the culmination of your life's experiences and is about rebirth and resurrection.

## REVERSED

This indicates wasted opportunities, indecision leading to delay, fear of the unknown, postponement of results, guilt, and blame. This is an inspiring card. It indicates that higher energies are in motion to assist us in living a new, fresh, and wonderful life. The card urges you to take renewed decisions as new doors are opening – an awakening to a new possibility.

## JYOTHI – THE SAGA

*Param-Jyothi* is the Supreme Light, the higher splendour of realisation, the merging of one's 'imagined self' into the universal self. It is the 'Way' of the Buddha that teaches man to feel what is beyond, and thus, to be freed from being imprisoned in any temporal aspect of life. When man achieves *Nirvana,* he will be able to see how everything is integrated into one whole. One must transcend suffering and must cease the cycle of arising and cessation, to become one with the Absolute, to walk the same path as the Buddha, to attain *Param-Jyothi.* The imagery of light is extraordinarily prevalent in many of the Buddhist scriptures.

—XXI—

THE WORLD ▪ brahman

*The* Trimurti *in this hand-painted illustration is a concept in Hinduism in which the cosmic functions of creation, maintenance, and destruction are personified as one. The identification of Vishnu, Shiva, and Brahma as one being is strongly emphasised in the Puranas, wherein Brahman is worshipped as the* Trimurti.

# THE WORLD ▪ brahman (XXI)

## THE CARD – THE INTERPRETATION

With the appearance of the *Brahman* / World card, the life cycle started by the Fool has come to an end. It is a time of achievement, success, happiness, and of course, endings. Similar in appearance to the Wheel of Fortune, the World is a card of balance with your inner and outer realities. On a more mundane level, the card embodies the completion of a long, sometimes difficult, journey. It signifies a sense of wholeness, dynamic balance, realisation of your goals, prosperity, and seeing your dreams come true.

## REVERSED

*Brahman* / the World card, being the last card in the deck of cards, symbolises the end of the journey as being the natural conclusion of life. The spiritual goal of a Hindu is to become one with *Brahman.* This freedom is referred to as *moksha* (salvation from the never-ending cycle of life). Until salvation is achieved, a Hindu believes that he/she will be repeatedly reincarnated in order that he/she may work towards self-realisation of the truth (the truth being that only *Brahman* exists).

## BRAHMAN – THE SAGA

As the source of *Dharma,* the metaphysical ordering principles inherent in the design of the cosmos, *Brahman* can be viewed as the Absolute Truth, as the final goal of all reality; *Brahman* is also the Final Cause. Being the source of all reality, *Brahman* is the only substantial truth that exists.

Chapter 4

# HOW TO READ TAROT CARDS

A few years ago, tarot cards would have conjured up images of gypsies. Today, the cards are popular among occultists and New Agers in all walks of life. The modern tarot deck has been traced back to 15th century Italy and a game called 'triumphs' (tarots in French; Decker, 1996). Millions of people seek tarot readings to help them in their daily lives. They ask about how to deal with their relationships and how to find success in their endeavours. Throughout history, people have turned to divination methods and communication with spiritual energies to help them and because tarot reading has been used for centuries now, it is often a trusted modern tool as well. Today, the benefits of tarot used as a tool of self-discovery are becoming clear. It is being used by counsellors and therapists, and indeed, many tarot readers – or consultants – are being turned to in a similar capacity. Readers often look for a deeper insight into their lives, and ideas for making positive change. There are several aspects of tarot card reading that make up its effectiveness. If all the conditions are met properly, the outcome of a tarot reading can be very effective.

## The Approach to Reading the Indian Spreads

The *Chakra* Spread and the *Karma* Spread are specially created keeping in mind the holistic approach to life in India. While the *Chakra* Spread embodies the elements of the spirit, the mind and the body, the *Karma* Spread works on the principle of *Karma* as a regenerative cycle of life. Keep an open mind as you read the messages in the cards and relate them to your own life. The tarot is indeed a powerful tool for you to use for guidance. To benefit from these readings, be open to the message given by the cards to vitalise and enrich your life. The cards of the Major Arcana refer to spiritual matters and important trends in the querent's life. You can either read the interpretation of the card to see how it fits in with the positioning or relate to the archetype on the card. The meaning of any card is modified according to whether or not it is upside down, its position in the spread, and the meaning of adjacent cards.

## How to Deal a Spread

Start by thinking of your question while you shuffle the deck, then with your left hand, cut the deck into three piles moving in a leftward direction.

Still using your left hand, pick up the pile on your right and place it on the centre pile and place this on the left pile. Pick up this combined pile and fan the cards in front of you. Keeping the question in your mind, pick out random cards from the pile of cards in front of you. A meditative frame of mind can be created by invoking the divine powers of the universe with a little prayer that you do on a daily basis.

## THE CHAKRA SPREAD

This spread would be more suited to someone looking for a meditative spread; each *chakra* represents a power centre on the body. Shuffle the cards and place the card on each *chakra* point. Each *chakra* point correlates to the levels of consciousness, archetypal elements, developmental stages of life, body functions, and much more. Simply draw one card for each *chakra* and place according to the spread layout. I find this spread very effective for focusing my attention to my inner state of mind and to my physical being.

## HOW TO INTERPRET A CHAKRA SPREAD

Shuffle the cards and place the cards on each *chakra* point according to the spread shown on the facing page.

Open the cards and read the card in reference to each *chakra* point. So for instance, if you get the Emperor in the first *chakra* point – the card could be interpreted as the following:

> The *Mooladhara chakra* indicates our basic survival instincts, our sense of grounding to our bodies in the physical plane. Since you have pulled out the Emperor card for this point, the card indicates an inherent leadership quality that will help you to accomplish and fulfil all that you desire. A card of authority, you are physically disciplined and grounded to deal with the change that will lead to new and better things. Read each card in reference to the *chakra* point and then interpret the meaning of the card according to the point it is placed on.

1. *Mooladhara Chakra* / Root Chakra

2. *Swadhisthan Chakra* / Sacral Chakra

3. *Manipura Chakra* / Solar Plexus Chakra

4. *Anahata Chakra* / The Heart Chakra

5. *Vishuddha Chakra* / Throat Chakra

6. *Ajna Chakra* / Brow *Chakra* / Third Eye

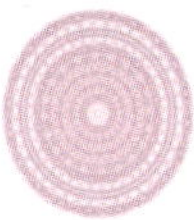

7. *Sahasrara Chakra* / Crown Chakra

## 1. MOOLADHARA CHAKRA *(Root / Base* Chakra)

The Base or Root *Chakra* is located at the very bottom of the spine. This *chakra* is the grounding force that allows us to connect to the earth energies and empower our being. This card indicates our survival instincts and forms the very foundation of our physical being. In a spread, this card will denote the querent's physical health, self-esteem, and zest for life.

**REVERSED:** If the card is reversed, there will be problems encountered in day-to-day life that will prevent us from moving. If the root *chakra* has too much energy flowing through it, this could cause selfishness, greed, an overpowering manner, irritation, aggression, and sadism. If there is too little energy flowing through it, this possibly will cause anxiety, lack of confidence, and a lack of ability to complete things.

## 2. SWADHISTHAN CHAKRA *(Sacral* Chakra)

The second *chakra* is located in the lower back/abdomen/sexual organs and is related to emotions and sexuality. The card is about friendliness, creativity, sexuality, emotions, and intuition. It connects us to others through feeling, desire, sensation, and movement. This card represents the querent's area of interest, creativity, sexuality, and strong emotions. It also reveals the relationship we have with those who bring out our strong emotional and sexual feelings.

**REVERSED:** If the card is reversed, it causes negative influences in the physical, in the form of emotional problems or sexual guilt, excesses in food, sex, and drugs. If this *chakra* has too much energy moving through it, we may become self-centred and too ambitious, jealous, distrusting, and cold.

## 3. MANIPURA CHAKRA *(Solar Plexus* Chakra*)*

This *chakra* is known as the power *chakra,* located in the solar plexus. The card rules our personal power, will, autonomy, and our metabolism. This shows where our power lies, or what makes us feel powerful, not necessarily in domination, but in establishing the core strength in life. The power position is all about energy, effectiveness, spontaneity, and non-dominating power.

**REVERSED:** If the card is reversed, it can lead to anger and frustration, as well as problems dealing with power and authority. It also indicates stubbornness and an inability to understand the real issues or challenges that confront you.

## 4. ANAHATA CHAKRA *(The Heart* Chakra*)*

This *chakra* is called the heart *chakra* and is the middle *chakra* in a system of seven. This card is related to the ability to love and harmonise all polarities in our being. A healthy fourth *chakra* allows us to love deeply, feel compassion, and have a deep sense of peace and centredness.

**REVERSED:** If the card is reversed, it can cause us to become unstable and emotionally cold and uncaring.

## 5. VISHUDDHA CHAKRA *(The Throat* Chakra*)*

This is the *chakra* located in the throat and is thus related to communication and creativity. This card influences communication, dreaming, artistic expression, good judgement, self-belief, wisdom, truthfulness, and our relationship with those who stimulate our ability to communicate. Physically, it influences the mouth, teeth, throat, thyroid gland, and the immune system.

**REVERSED:** If the card is reversed, it can make us inflexible, dominating, egotistical, big-headed, causing us to have a self-righteous attitude. This chakra is about living and expressing our own truth. It is also about taking responsibility and the risk to be who you really want to be.

## 6. AJNA CHAKRA *(The Brow* Chakra / *Third Eye)*

This *chakra* is known as the brow *chakra* or third eye centre. This card represents vision, insight, intuition, concentration, imagination, and clairvoyance. As such, it reveals our psychic faculties and our understanding of archetypal levels. When healthy, it allows us to be without judgement embracing ourselves unconditionally.

**REVERSED:** If the energy flow is too great, it can cause a lack of concentration, headaches, making us confused, causing spiritual fatigue, psychological problems or panic attacks, and depression. When there is a lack of energy, it can cause us to be disorderly, unassertive, frightened of achieving, too sensitive to the feelings of others, and unaware of what comes from the self or from our highest guidance.

## 7. SAHASRARA CHAKRA *(The Crown* Chakra*)*

This is the crown *chakra* that relates to consciousness as pure awareness. This card indicates our connection to the greater world beyond, to a timeless, spaceless place of all-knowing. This *chakra* denotes knowledge, wisdom, understanding, and spiritual connection to the universe and all that abides in it.

**REVERSED:** If the card is reversed, our ego will influence our actions. This can cause us to become unsure of ourselves, reducing our self-confidence and creating fear and anxiety. It can create negative influences which can be seen in the form of lack of inspiration, confusion, depression, alienation, self-denial, and a need for sympathy.

Look at all the cards and how they relate to one another. The *chakras* are all dependent on each other to work in harmony and balance. Always remember, a *chakra* reading is NOT a definitive answer or prediction as to what actions you should take. It is a tool to help you better understand your state of mind and to bring out things that may lie in your unconscious, or perhaps things that are either out of your control or hidden from you in some way. Use the *chakra* spread to understand your inner fears and areas in your life that need to be reinforced.

## THE KARMIC SPREAD

The *Karmic* Spread offers intuitive insight into the purpose of our life and the life patterns associated with our numerous births and rebirths. The *Karmic* spread offers you an opportunity to understand your life blockages and help you to lead a healthier and more peaceful life. Once you understand your *Karmic* goals, you can exercise free will. The *Karmic* wheel represents the eight-fold teachings of the Buddha. Although all things are impermanent, all occurrences in one's life are conditioned by others. One event, action, or reaction, results in an effect and that in turn causes other events, actions, and reactions. In order to get off the '*Karmic* Wheel' one must initiate the correct moral action to free oneself from the never-ending cycle of life.

1 2 3 4 5 6 7 8 9

1. Main *Karmic* lesson you brought into this life
2. Past-life patterns / emotions that necessitated the lesson
3. Present status or challenges you face in your life
4. Challenges you will face in the future
5. *Karmic* lesson to learn
6. Attitude or emotions required to achieve *Karmic* goal
7. Your *Karmic* gift
8. *Karmic* goal in this life
9. A *Karmic* gift

## Some Common Card Spreads

### ONE CARD SPREAD

This is the easiest means of divining an answer; you have only to look at a single card. Shuffle the cards while thinking of your question, then intuitively pick out one card and turn it over. The card will give you an overall situation relevant to the question.

### THREE-CARDS SPREAD

This three-card spread links you to the earth below and heaven above. A short meditative reading, it helps you to get an amazing understanding of the situation in the past, present, and future. One of the most effective spreads, I use this most often for my readings.

Past Present Future

### CARD PLACEMENT

This card represents the past or the basis of the matter. It explains the events, circumstances, or conditions that have led up to where you are now.

**Card 1:** *Past influences:* This card represents the past, the basis of the matter. It reveals the circumstances in the past leading to the current situation. **Card 2:** *This card represents the present.* It represents the present or general theme of the querent's situation. **Card 3:** *The future:* This card represents your future and reveals the end result or the outcome of the situation.

## FIVE-CARDS SPREAD

The five positions of this spread look at the flow of events in time. This spread will help you track unfolding issues and possible consequences.

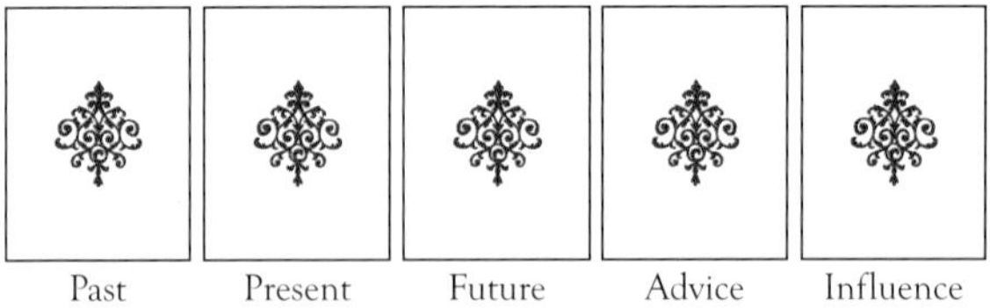


Card 1: *Past influences still having effect*
Card 2: *The present or general theme of the reading*
Card 3: *The future*
Card 4: *The reason behind the question (this will probably shed light on 2)*
Card 5: *The potential within the situation*

This is a very useful spread when trying to decide a given course of action. Card 4 will often reveal a subconscious impulse – perhaps a blockage which is stopping you from achieving your desired result. Card 5 shows the possible results from following a given course of action. The card works best if, whilst selecting the card, you concentrate on the outcome of the situation rather than the question.

## THE CELTIC CROSS

A full Celtic cross reading delivers powerful insights, advice, and predictions touching on several aspects of your life, and how those parts interact. The ten positions of the Celtic cross offer enough detail to represent complex situations, which is why it has been the standard tarot spread for hundreds of years.

## LAYOUT AND PROCEDURE

**1.** Shuffle the cards while thinking of your question. **2.** With your left hand, cut the deck into three piles moving in a leftward direction. **3.** Still using your left hand, pick up the pile on your right and place it over the centre pile. **4.** Pick up this combined pile, and place it on the last. **5.** With your left hand, lay ten cards face up in the positions shown in the diagram. **6.** Each position has a particular significance as explained below.

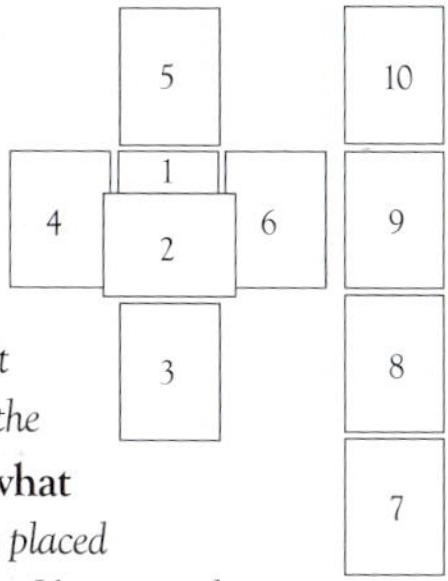


## CARD PLACEMENT

**1. This is what encompasses you.** *It represents the general atmosphere and the querent's main thought process.* **2. This is what crosses you for the good or ill.** *This card is placed sideways over #1. This represents opposing forces. If it is a good card, it will help the present situation.* **3. This is what represents your core.** *This card represents what brought the situation about, the foundation of your being.* **4. This is what's behind you.** *This represents what has just happened, or the influences that are passing away.* **5. This is what crowns you.** *The current situation and influences.* **6. This is what is before you.** *This card represents what will happen in the very near future if the querent continues on their current path.* **7. This card represents you innermost fears.** *Negative feelings about fears.* **8. The thoughts of those around you.** *Depicts the opinions and influences of friends and family.* **9. The querent's hopes.** *Reveals the querent's own hopes and aspirations.* **10. Outcome:** *This card tells what the overall final outcome will be if the querent continues on his/her current path.*

CHAPTER 5

# ABOUT THE DECK

| INDIAN NAME | MEANING |
|---|---|
| 0. vidhushak | The *vidhushak* is a blend of the clown of Sanskrit plays and a folk performer in Indian mythology. The *Vidhushak* is a *natgiri*, a vagabond, and a wise character who delivers a constructive message to society in a light and spiritual vein. |
| I. usha | She is the life and health of all things, being born every day and yet she is an immortal being. *Usha*, the Goddess of Dawn, is the daughter of Heaven. She symbolises the awakening consciousness and the power of truth and clarity. |
| II. shakti | Shakti is the Mother Goddess, the source of all, the universal principle of energy, power, or creativity. |
| III. shasthi | Shasthi is the name of the Hindu Goddess of Fertility and Childbirth. She is the goddess for gifting children. |
| IV. purusha | In Hindu mythology, *purusha* is the cosmic man, having a thousand heads, a thousand eyes, a thousand feet encompassing the earth, spreading in all directions into animate and inanimate things. |
| V. atman | *Atman* is a philosophical term used in Hinduism to identify the soul. The word '*atman*' originally meant 'breath' or 'soul' or 'vital principle' (as the word '*atmen*' does in German). *Atman* is the individual soul. In essence it is but a minuscule form of *Brahman*, self-merging with the absolute universality of *Brahman*. |
| VI. purus and prakriti | Radha and Krishna, the eternal lovers symbolise the union of '*purus* and *prakriti*'. *Purus* is the individual soul and *prakriti* represents the absolute universe. |
| VII. rath | Chariots are an important part of Hindu mythology, with most of the gods in their pantheon portrayed as riding them. Chariots figure prominently in the *Rig Veda*, establishing their presence in India as early as in the second millennium BC. There is also reference to Krishna, the charioteer, in the epic, the Mahabharata, giving a life sermon to Arjuna, which constitutes the teaching of the *Bhagavad Gita*. |

| VIII. bhima | One of the five Pandavas in the epic, the Mahabharata, Bhima is a legendary figure, a giant in physical strength, whose legendary prowess has been mentioned throughout the epic. Bhima was a pivotal figure in the great battle of Kurukshetra and his charioteer was Lord Krishna's son. Bhima was bestowed with a great mind and was supposed to be a strategist with superhuman strength. |
|---|---|
| IX. rishi | In Hinduism, a *rishi* is a sage and / or a seer who 'heard' the hymns of the Vedas from the Supreme Being – *Brahman* while he was in deep meditation. A *rishi* can be regarded as a combination of a patriarch, a priest, a preceptor, an author of Vedic hymns, a sage, a saint, and an ascetic. |
| X. dharma | The *Dharma Chakra,* wheel, is a symbol representing *Dharma* (law) in Buddhism and the teaching of the path to enlightenment. It is also sometimes translated as Wheel of Doctrine or Wheel of Law. The *Dharma Chakra* from the Lion Capital of Ashoka, at Sarnath, is the national emblem of India and is also shown on the flag of India. It represents *Dharma, i.e.,* natural conduct of a nation. |
| XI. nyaya | *Nyaya* or Hindu logic was founded by Gautama *Rishi,* also known by the names Akshapada and Dirghatapas. *Nyaya* is an analytic type of philosophy. The word '*nyaya*' signifies going into a subject, *i.e.,* investigating it analytically. In this sense of analysis, the word '*nyaya*' is exactly opposed to *Sankhya,* synthesis. *Nyaya* is sometimes called *Tarka-Vidya* or the Science of Debate, *Vada-Vidya* or the Science of Discussion. *Tarka* is the special feature of *nyaya.* |
| XII. tyaga | *Tyaga* or renunciation in Hindu mythology denotes a gradual dissociation from worldly objects and from the seed of desire. This renunciation is not a renunciation of something material but is closer to the notion of ascetic renunciation. *Tyaga* also involves giving up the fruits of action and performing *Karma* without expecting any fruit for such action. |
| XIII. yama | *Yama* is the God of Death and the embodiment of the rule of law and imparts justice according to the deeds of each person. He is to uphold justice and is an adjudicator after death. *Dharma* is the law or way of the universe or cosmos. With this extra duty he was given the title of *Dharma-Raja* or Lord of *Dharma.* |

| | |
|---|---|
| XIV. ardhnarishvara | *Yoga* is part of the intentional effort humans can perform to rejoin with the source, or *Brahman*. *Yoga* is the 'union' of the individual with the infinite. It is also balance, adaptation, and adjustment, resulting in equilibrium. This is tempering the soul to make it a fit vessel for higher illumination. |
| XV. asura | *Asura*, from Sanskrit, meaning a 'power-seeking' and 'power-hungry' being, described as a 'demon'; or *anaya* (non-Aryan) people of ancient India. In Indian mythology, the *danavas*, *asuras*, *daityas* (synonyms) of Hindu mythology are not bad individually. They worship Gods (mostly Shiva). Ravana was a great devotee of Shiva. Many others got boons from Shiva or Brahma, but they are never known to worship Vishnu. They keep their promises, respect women. But they are eternal enemies of *suras*, *devas*, *adityas* (synonyms again). *Asuras* have no particular enmity for humans but humans get caught in their cross-fire with *Devas*, more so because humans side with *Devas*. |
| XVI. kila | The *Kilas* of India form an important part of Indian History. They are architectural marvels that relate to interesting facts and events that form an integral part of Indian folklore. |
| XVII. tara | Goddess Tara is one among the oldest Hindu goddesses still worshipped widely. She is the symbol of peace and protection. She is the also the great goddess of Tibetan Buddhism. Like Kali, she can be viewed as the devouring Star who consumes wicked unbelievers, or as the light, which leads the good when they are threatened by evil forces. |
| XVIII. chandra | *Soma* is the Moon God also known as *Chandra*. According to a legend, *Surya* nourishes the moon with water from the ocean when *Soma* is exhausted by the many beings that feed upon his substance. It is believed that during half the month, thirty-six thousand divinities feed on *Soma* and thus assure their immortality. |
| XIX. surya | The Sun God, who is also known as Narayana, or Vishnu, the soul of all the worlds, is situated in outer space between the upper and lower portions of the universe. As the source of light, *Surya* / the Sun is the most readily apparent image of divinity available to man. |

| | |
|---|---|
| XX. jyothi | *Param-Jyothi*: the Supreme Light, the higher splendour of realisation, merging his 'imagined self' into the Universal Self. The word *Jyothi* (Light) does not connote the physical light of the material world. |
| XXI. brahman | As the source of *Dharma,* the metaphysical ordering principles inherent in the design of the cosmos, *Brahman* can be viewed as the Absolute Truth, as the final goal of all reality; *Brahman* is also the Final Cause. Being the source of all reality, *Brahman* is the only substantial truth that exists. |

# Chapter 6

# Table of Correspondence

# Table Of Correspondence

| CARD NUMBER | NORDIC NAME | INDIAN NAME | MEANING |
|---|---|---|---|
| 0 | The Fool | vidhushak | Innocence, unrealised potential, life journey. |
| I | The Magician | usha | Mastery, self-confidence. |
| II | The High Priestess | shakti | Mysteries, hidden meanings. |
| III | The Empress | shasthi | Fertility, creativity. |
| IV | The Emperor | purusha | Authority, leadership. |
| V | The Hierophant | atman | High level of development and growth.The merging of earth-water-fire-air-ether. |
| VI | The Lovers | purus and prakriti | Harmonisation of all dualities, a union. |
| VII | The Chariot | rath | Success, overcoming all obstacles, achievement. |
| VIII | Strength | bhima | Strength of character, bravery facing incredible odds, self-worth and confidence. |
| IX | The Hermit | rishi | Spiritual guidance, choosing a solitary path, withdrawal into self. |
| X | The Wheel of Fortune | dharma | Completion of a cycle, luck, easy-come-easy-go. |
| XI | Justice | nyaya | Fair conclusion of matter, successful legal dealings. |
| XII | The Hanged Man | tyaga | Pausing to contemplate or meditate, acceptance of one's situation, sacrifice for a higher good. |
| XIII | Death | yama | Rebirth, transformation, ending, transition, elimination. |
| XIV | Temperance | ardh-narishvara | Moderation, blending of opposites. |
| XV | The Devil | asura | Bound to a particular idea, obsession, and manipulation of others. |

| XVI | THE TOWER | kila | Sudden and drastic changes in one's life. Disruptions leading to personal transformation. |
|---|---|---|---|
| XVII | THE STAR | tara | Inspiration, understanding, hope, courage. |
| XVIII | THE MOON | chandra | Imagination, intuition, delusion. Uncovering what is in the unconscious. |
| XIX | THE SUN | surya | Success, optimism, bright outlook. Can also mean material happiness or a successful marriage of a brilliant child. |
| XX | THE JUDGEMENT | jyothi | Awakening, often of a spiritual nature. Change of position in life or outlook. |
| XXI | THE WORLD | brahman | Success in undertakings, culmination of the life journey. |

## BIBLIOGRAPHY

Arthur, Edward. *The Original Raider Waite Tarot Pack,* U.S. Games Systems, 1993.

Crowley, Aleister. *Book of Thoth (Egyptian Tarot),* U.S. Games Systems Inc., 1972.

——. *Tarot Divination,* Samuel Weiser, New York, 1976.

Gearhart, Sally, and Susan Rennie. *A Feminist Tarot,* Persephone Press, Watertown, Massachusettes, 1981.

Jayanti, Amber. *Living the Tarot,* Wordsworth Editions, Hertfordshire, England, 2000.

Low Australian National University, 1997.

Marchett, Ciro. *The Gilded Tarot,* Llewellyn Publications, Florida, 2004.

Milo, Lon. Aleister Crowley: *Understanding Aleister Crowley's Thoth Tarot,* Weiser LLC, 2003.

Nichols, Sallie. *Marseilles Tarot: Jung & Tarot: An Archetypal Journey,* Weiser, 1980.

Ouspensky, P.D. *The Symbolism of the Tarot,* Dover Publications, New York, 1976.

Walker, Barbara G. *The Secrets of the Tarot: Origins, History and Symbolism,* Harper, San Francisco, 1984.

Wanless, James. *New Age Tarot,* Fair Winds Press, 2008.

William, David. *The Fool's Journey: A Semiotic Heuristic for the Greenie Genre 1,*

## WEBSITES

http://www.aeclectic.net/tarot/
http://www.britannica.com/
http://www.encyclopediaofauthentichinduism.org/
http://en.wikipedia.org
http://www.experiencefestival.com/~Globaloneness.com
http://www.hinduismnet.com
http://www.hindupedia.com/en/Main_Page
http://www.hinduism.co.za/
http://www.indiadivine.org
http://www.indianculture online.com
http://www.tarotcollectors.com/
http://www.tarotforum.net/
http://www.tarotpedia.com
http://www.tarotteachings.com/three-of-wands.html
http://www.thefreedictionary.com

MY TRYST WITH THE TAROT BEGAN AROUND TWENTY YEARS AGO, WHEN I WAS INTRODUCED TO THESE BY A FAMOUS PSYCHIC AND TAROT READER WAY BACK IN EAST AFRICA.

Drawn to the esoteric, my experience with tarot cards has been wonderfully positive, empowering, and helping me connect with the most essential parts of my being. Spiritually also, the tarot played a crucial part in selecting my life path. Over the years, I have come to believe that life is an adventure, and we are constantly given opportunities to connect to our inner self and to learn from these challenges. I have regularly used the tarot as a tool for self-exploration and have also helped friends seek a fresh understanding of a situation.

Fascinated by the tarot symbology, I have explored various decks and found esoteric similarities in the symbols used in all the decks. This inspired me to put together an Indian deck of cards, replacing the classic tarot archetypes with Indian figures and symbolism. The cards took me nearly two years to complete and I hope this mosaic of Indian cards put together by a group of upcoming Indian artists will be enjoyed by a broad spectrum of people.

I am a member of various online tarot forums, blogs and communities. I enjoy discussing all aspects of the tarot with a group of tarot collectors, readers and enthusiasts worldwide and am a member of the Aeclectic Tarot Forum, Tarotpedia Forum Community, Lotus Tarot Forum, and the Tarot History Forum.

Visit *The Sacred Indian Tarot* Blog and leave your comments:
**www.thesacredindiantarot.blogspot.com/**

An online interactive version of *The Sacred Indian Tarot* can be found at **www.ombooks.com.**
For any further queries, please contact the author at **krai99@yahoo.com.**
Zoë Collington, the Creative Designer, can be contacted at **zoecollington@gmail.com.**

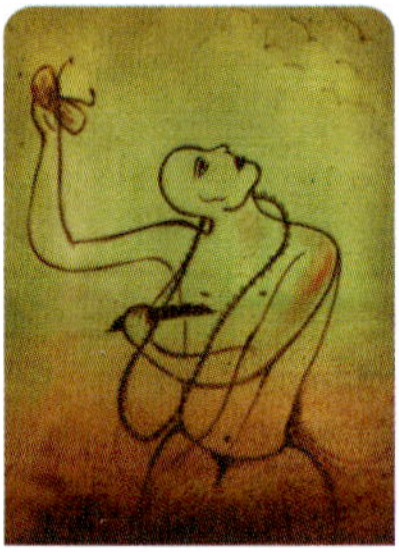

THE FOOL - vidhushak

THE MAGICIAN - usha

THE HIGH PRIESTESS - shakti

THE EMPRESS - shasthi

THE EMPEROR - purusha

THE HIEROPHANT - atman

THE LOVERS - purus and prakriti

THE CHARIOT - rath

STRENGTH - bhima

THE HERMIT - rishi

THE WHEEL OF FORTUNE - dharma

JUSTICE - nyaya

THE HANGED MAN - tyaga

DEATH - yama

TEMPERANCE - ardhnarishvara

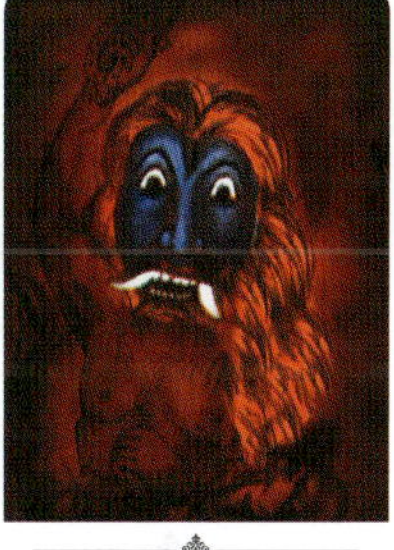

THE DEVIL - asura

THE TOWER - kila

THE STAR - tara

THE MOON - chandra

THE SUN - surya

THE JUDGEMENT - jyothi

THE WORLD - brahman